January 1

January 1

JANUARY 1

January 1

January 1

A Happy New Year

1 JANUARY

PLATE 1 *New Year's Day*

PLATE 2 *Valentine's Day*

TO MY SWEETHEART.

MY HEART'S DEAREST.

With love to my LOVE.

Baby Cupid is a rogue
With his tender charm,
Tells you, kisses are in vogue,
Will not do you harm;
But sweet Valentine, beware!
Love brings joy,
but also care.

PLATE 3 *Valentine's Day*

PLATE 4   *Valentine's Day*

PLATE 5 *Saint Patrick's Day*

PLATE 6 *Saint Patrick's Day*

PLATE 7 *Saint Patrick's Day*

PLATE 8   *Easter*

PLATE 9   *Easter*

EASTER GREETING

PLATE 10 *Easter*

PLATE 11 *Independence Day*

PLATE 12 *Independence Day*

PLATE 14 *Halloween*

PLATE 15 *Halloween*

PLATE 16 *Halloween*

Thanksgiving Joys

PLATE 17 *Thanksgiving*

PLATE 18   *Thanksgiving*

PLATE 19 *Thanksgiving*

Within the illustrations:

TAKE ONE

DO YOUR CHRISTMAS SHOPPING EARLY

MAY YOUR CHRISTMAS BE BRIGHT AND HAPPY

PLATE 20 *Christmas*

Do Your
Xmas Shopping Early.

DECEMBER
25
Christmas Day

Do your
Christmas
Shopping
Early.

PLATE 21 *Christmas*

PLATE 24 *Christmas*

PLATE 23   *Christmas*

PLATE 22 *Christmas*